A TRUE BOOK

Insects and Spiders

CHRISTINE TAYLOR-BUTLER

Children's Press®
An Imprint of Scholastic Inc.
New York   Toronto   London   Auckland   Sydney
Mexico City   New Delhi   Hong Kong
Danbury, Connecticut

Content Consultant
Stephen S. Ditchkoff, PhD
Professor of Wildlife Sciences
Auburn University
Auburn, Alabama

Library of Congress Cataloging-in-Publication Data
Taylor-Butler, Christine.
Insects and spiders / by Christine Taylor-Butler.
pages cm. — (A true book)
Includes bibliographical references and index.
Audience: Ages 9–12.
Audience: Grades 4–6.
ISBN 978-0-531-21753-5 (lib. bdg.) — ISBN 978-0-531-22338-3 (pbk.)
1. Insects—Juvenile literature. 2. Spiders—Juvenile literature. I. Title.
QL467.2.T395 2013
595.4'4—dc23   2013002137

No part of this publication may be reproduced in whole or in part, or stored in a retrieval system, or transmitted in any form or by any means, electronic, mechanical, photocopying, recording, or otherwise, without written permission of the publisher. For information regarding permission, write to Scholastic Inc., Attention: Permissions Department, 557 Broadway, New York, NY 10012. © 2014 Scholastic Inc.

All rights reserved. Published in 2014 by Children's Press, an imprint of Scholastic Inc.
Printed in China 62
SCHOLASTIC, CHILDREN'S PRESS, A TRUE BOOK™, and associated logos are trademarks and/or registered trademarks of Scholastic Inc.
7 8 9 10 R 23 22 21 20 19 18

Scholastic Inc., 557 Broadway, New York, NY 10012.

Front cover: Blue dragonfly
Front cover inset: Jumping spider
Back cover: Leaf-cutter ants in Costa Rica, Central America

Find the Truth!

Everything you are about to read is true *except* for one of the sentences on this page.

Which one is **TRUE**?

T or F   Insects are a good source of nutrition.

T or F   Spiders go through a process called metamorphosis.

Find the answers in this book.

Contents

1 Life in the Field

Does a tarantula share something with a
leaf-cutter ant and a monarch butterfly? 7

2 It's Classified

How many segments do insect
and spider bodies have? 11

3 Millions of Homes in Millions of Places

What materials do insects use to build their homes? . . 21

THE BIG TRUTH!

Disappearing Act

What is happening to honeybees
in the United States? 28

4

**Common red
soldier beetle**

4 Circle of Life

How many stages do most insects
experience as they mature?.................... **31**

5 Friend or Foe?

How have insects led to human hunger? **39**

True Statistics........... **44**

Resources **45**

Important Words........ **46**

Index **47**

About the Author........ **48**

Only female mosquitoes
suck blood.

Life in the Field

Millions of tiny leaf-cutter ants march across a field, carrying leaf segments. They chew up the leaves and deposit them in a fungus garden. There, the plants will decay into food for the colony. Other tiny workers in the colony have a different task. Soldiers protect the nest. Others tend the garden. The largest, the queen, will lay millions of eggs. Found mostly in Central and South America, these leaf-cutter ants may be the world's oldest farmers.

 Leaf-cutter ants can carry more than 50 times their body weight.

Poisonous Predator

Large and hairy, a tarantula spins a strand of silk in front of its home and then lies in wait for prey. A cricket crosses the thread, which signals the tarantula that its meal has arrived. The spider strikes, injecting the cricket with poison from its two venomous fangs. The poison turns the inside of the cricket to liquid, which the spider drinks. Tarantulas may look scary, but their bite won't hurt most people.

A tarantula's hairs can break off and irritate a predator.

Each generation of monarch butterflies migrates either south or north. No generation makes both trips.

A Long Journey

Each fall, millions of monarch butterflies migrate more than 3,000 miles (4,828 kilometers) to escape the cold northern winter. They travel from Canada to Mexico, feasting on milkweed plants along the way. In Mexico, these large orange and black butterflies reproduce before dying. The next generation of butterflies will migrate north in the spring.

These animals all have something in common. Can you guess what it is?

Arthropods, including grasshoppers, tend to be smaller than warm-blooded animals, such as birds or mammals.

CHAPTER 2

It's Classified

These animals are all arthropods. But what exactly is an arthropod? Arthropods are cold-blooded. Because they are cold-blooded, they can't regulate their body temperature. Their body temperature is the same as the environment around them. Arthropods are also invertebrates. This means their segmented bodies have no backbones.

Insects and spiders are two common types of arthropods. There are millions of arthropod species on Earth.

The word *arthropod* is Latin for "having a jointed foot."

Understanding Arthropods

Scientists who study insects and spiders are called entomologists. They use a system of classification to keep track of all animal species. It is similar to a family tree. Arthropods are found in the invertebrate branch of the chart. Arthropods with similar characteristics are grouped into classes.

Insects are members of the class Insecta. Spiders belong to the class Arachnida.

An entomologist collects moths and other insects on a sheet, having attracted them with the light of a lamp.

Quick Facts About Common Arthropods

Group (number of species)	Characteristics	Diet	Distribution	Life Span
Insects (925,000 cataloged, 10 million estimated)	Ominivorous, eating both plants and meat	Egg layers; go through **metamorphosis**, or transformation as they mature	Found on every continent	30 minutes (mayfly) to several years (bees and ants) Note: Mayflies live less than a day as adults, but spend 1–3 years as **naiads**, or underdeveloped young
Butterflies (20,000)	Herbivorous, or plant eater: nectar from flowers, fluid from rotting fruit	Egg layers; go through metamorphosis	Found on every continent except Antarctica	2–6 weeks in the adult stage; eggs can hibernate for several months
Moths (120,000)	Herbivorous: nectar from flowers, grains, natural fibers such as cotton and wool	Egg layers; go through metamorphosis	Found on every continent except Antarctica	2–5 weeks in the adult stage; total life span, including **larvae** and adult stages, 1 year
Spiders (40,000 or more)	Carnivorous, or meat eater: mostly insects and other spiders	Lay eggs that hatch into complete spiders	Found on every continent except Antarctica	1–2 years for most; tarantulas up to 20 years

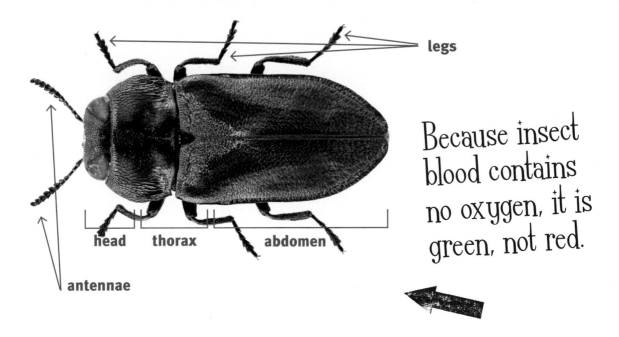

legs

head   thorax   abdomen

antennae

Because insect blood contains no oxygen, it is green, not red.

Class Insecta

Insects have some common characteristics. For example, most have three pairs of legs. Their bodies are divided into three parts: the head, the thorax, and the abdomen. The head contains the eyes, brain, mouth, and antennae. The thorax contains the muscles, wings, and legs. The abdomen contains the stomach, intestines, and reproductive organs. Insects have no lungs. Instead, they exchange oxygen through special cells on the thorax and abdomen.

An insect's body is protected by a hard multi-layered shell called an **exoskeleton**. It is made of a substance called **chitin**. The top layer is waxy and water-resistant. An insect's body also has symmetry. If you drew a line down the middle, from head to abdomen, the two halves would be mirror images of each other. There are more than 925,000 known species of insects. Some have wings, including bees, ants, beetles, flies, and grasshoppers.

The common red soldier beetle flies from plant to plant in search of smaller insects to eat.

Butterflies and Moths

Butterflies and moths are also members of the Insecta class. They are characterized by four large wings covered with tiny scales. Both moths and butterflies have antennae, which they use to smell. Butterflies rely more on sight than smell. They have slender antennae with hooks or clubs on the ends. But a moth's antennae are often feathery, with more sensors. This provides a better sense of smell as a moth flies through the dark night.

The large spots on an Io moth's wings can look like eyes, scaring away potential predators by making them think the "eyes" belong to a much bigger animal.

16

Pretty Predators

Ladybugs look pretty, but they also perform a very important function. They eat insects called aphids that are harmful to plants.

Farmers and gardeners often put ladybugs near crops or in a garden. Although they only live four to six weeks, a single ladybug can eat more than 5,000 bugs in its lifetime. Predators don't like ladybugs. Ladybugs secrete a fluid that makes them taste bad.

Class Arachnida

Spiders are not insects. They belong to the class Arachnida. Unlike insects, a spider's body is divided into two parts. And spiders have eight legs instead of six. Instead of antennae, spiders have fangs and a pair of appendages, called palps, for feeding and reproduction. Most spiders have eight eyes, although some have fewer. Even so, they don't see very well. They rely on touch, taste, and vibration to get around and find prey.

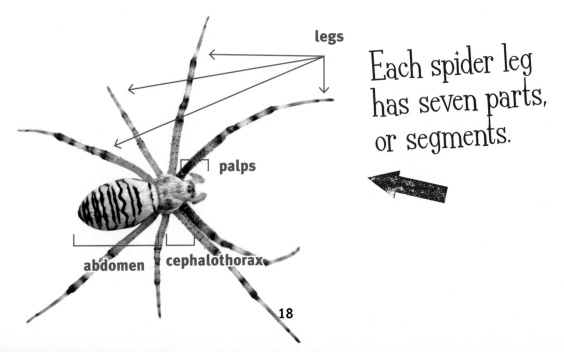

legs

palps

abdomen   cephalothorax

Each spider leg has seven parts, or segments.

18

Spider silk can be about five times stronger than piano wire.

Unlike insects, spiders use an organ called book lungs to breathe. Air passes across special plates and enters the spider's body. Arachnid blood cells do not carry oxygen the same way human blood does. That is why spider blood is blue in color.

Spiders have the rare ability to make silk. Spinnerets on their abdomen contain thousands of tubes that secrete liquid silk. They use this to build strong, sticky webs.

Scarab beetles can be a variety of colors. This metallic green scarab is native to the Amazon rain forest.

CHAPTER 3

Millions of Homes in Millions of Places

Insects and spiders are found in every part of the planet. They live in deserts, forests, urban areas, grasslands, and swamps. While adult insects don't live underwater, some, such as mosquitoes and dragonflies, breed in shallow, stagnant pools. Insects and spiders are small, but scientists have cataloged around 1 million species and believe there are millions more to be discovered.

 Insects make up 90 percent of animal species in the Amazon rainforest.

Being Social

Some insects are social and live in specialized groups called colonies. Each member of the colony has a certain function, such as guarding the queen, building the colony, or finding food.

Bees build hives made of a waxy substance. One hive can hold up to 40,000 bees. Wasps build

nests from wood fiber that they chew to make it soft. Sometimes the nests are made of mud.

Wasps, unlike some bees, can sting more than once.

Each colony of wasps dies off in winter. New colonies are born each spring.

Worker ants, which are always female, build an ant colony's home.

Other insects build their colonies in soil. Ants, for example, tunnel into the ground to create homes for breeding and storing food. They help the environment by eating dead insects and plant materials, distributing seeds, and helping **aerate** the soil. Other colonies, such as carpenter ants and termites, can be more destructive. They make their homes by tunneling through wood, which can damage homes and other property.

Fruit flies have a life span of about 8 to 10 days.

Flies

Flies are scavengers. Many species, such as the
housefly, feed on rotting fruit, garbage, dead
animals, and feces. They lay their eggs where larvae
can feed on the decaying matter. Hairs on flies'
bodies help them taste and smell their surroundings.
Sticky pads on their feet allow them to climb vertical
surfaces, such as windows. Flies help break down
organic substances in the environment. They can
also spread germs and disease.

Night and Day

Butterflies are diurnal—they come out during the day. Moths are usually nocturnal—they come out at night. Butterflies feed on nectar from flowers and fruit. Moths drink nectar, but they also like natural fibers, such as cotton and wool. That is why people sometimes find holes in their clothing. Farmers consider moths to be pests. These insects often slip into grain silos and help themselves to the food, damaging the farm's grain supply.

Hummingbird moths are unique among moths—they come out during the day.

Swarms and Spiderwebs

Grasshoppers prefer dry habitats with lots of grass. They're often found in deserts and scrub forests. They aren't hardy enough to survive a winter. Only their eggs can withstand the cold.

Grasshoppers are diurnal. They don't have nests, and they can travel 15 miles (24 km) a day to find food. Sometimes grasshoppers swarm in groups of thousands or millions. In those numbers, they can destroy a farm's entire crop.

Mild winters allow grasshoppers to thrive and multiply.

The thin strands of a spider's web can be difficult to spot in dense underbrush.

Spiders live everywhere except Antarctica. Although they prefer shelter and moisture, they can adapt to areas even where there is little or no water. Spider homes blend with their environment. Most people find spiders by locating their webs, which are made from strong strands of silk. Spiders are carnivorous predators. Many use their sticky webs to trap insects and small animals.

THE **BIG** TRUTH!

Disappearing Act

When people think of bees, they often think of honey. But bees play a more important role. They are responsible for pollinating more than one-third of the world's food crops.

However, whole colonies of bees have been disappearing without a trace at an alarming rate. This phenomenon is called colony collapse disorder. Scientists believe pesticides and genetically modified crops may be the problem. Both may poison or weaken the immune systems of bees. Other experts suspect a fungus or virus.

With more than 20,000 bee species at stake, scientists fear that the loss of crop pollinators will lead to dangerously few successful crops in the future.

WASHINGTON
MONTANA
NORTH DAKOTA
MINNESOTA
NEW HAMPSHIRE
VERMONT
MAINE
OREGON
IDAHO
SOUTH DAKOTA
WISCONSIN
MICHIGAN
NEW YORK
MASSACHUSETTS
WYOMING
NEBRASKA
IOWA
PENNSYLVANIA
RHODE ISLAND
CONNECTICUT
NEW JERSEY
NEVADA
UTAH
COLORADO
KANSAS
ILLINOIS
INDIANA
OHIO
WEST VIRGINIA
DELAWARE
MARYLAND
CALIFORNIA
MISSOURI
KENTUCKY
VIRGINIA
ARIZONA
NEW MEXICO
OKLAHOMA
ARKANSAS
TENNESSEE
NORTH CAROLINA
SOUTH CAROLINA
TEXAS
MISSISSIPPI
ALABAMA
GEORGIA
LOUISIANA
FLORIDA

North
West ✦ East
South

ALASKA

HAWAII

States reporting colony collapse disorder as of 2007

A human has 629 muscles in his or her body. A caterpillar has thousands.

CHAPTER 4

Circle of Life

Insects and spiders begin their life cycles as eggs. After hatching, insects go through a process called metamorphosis. This means their bodies go through several changes from the juvenile stage to the adult stage.

Spiders grow up differently. They do not go through metamorphosis. Spiders lay their eggs in soft sacs. The eggs hatch into fully formed baby spiders.

 Scientists believe that insects have been on Earth for almost 500 million years.

Complete Metamorphosis

Most insects, such as bees, ants, beetles, and flies, undergo complete metamorphosis. This process involves four stages: egg, larva, **pupa**, and adult. When fly eggs hatch, the larvae resemble tiny worms. They shed their exoskeletons, or molt, three times as they grow. The third larva skin forms a hard surface surrounding the insect. This is the pupal stage. The pupa grows into an adult and pushes its way out of the skin.

Butterfly larvae are called caterpillars. Some species of caterpillar can live on only one type of plant. Unlike other insects, which only molt three times as larvae, a caterpillar molts several times. Then it either spins a **chrysalis** or forms one under its skin. Inside the chrysalis, a caterpillar becomes a pupa and continues to change. After around two weeks, the insect breaks free as a fully formed butterfly.

From Egg to Butterfly

A female butterfly lays eggs on a leaf. Each species chooses one particular type of plant for its young.

The eggs hatch into caterpillars, which eat the plant. They molt several times as they grow.

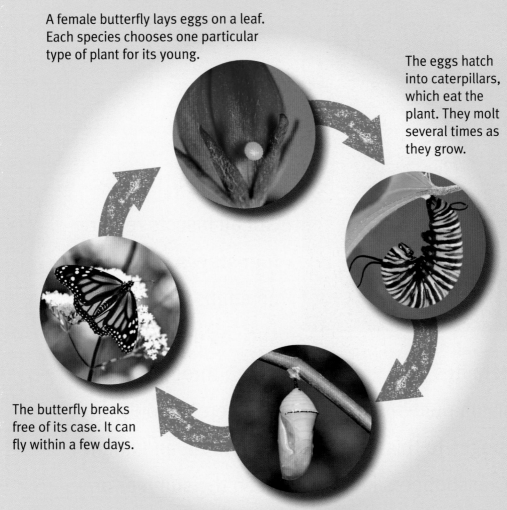

The butterfly breaks free of its case. It can fly within a few days.

The caterpillar's outer skin hardens into a chrysalis, and the larva becomes a pupa.

exoskeleton

This grasshopper has outgrown its exoskeleton, and so it is molting, revealing a new exoskeleton.

Incomplete Metamorphosis

Not all insects require four stages to become an adult. Some, such as dragonflies, termites, and grasshoppers, go through incomplete metamorphosis. There are only three stages to this process: egg, **nymph**, and adult. Grasshoppers lay their eggs in the summer or fall. The eggs hatch in the spring. The nymphs resemble a smaller version of the adult. They molt five times before becoming an adult.

There Are Always Exceptions

Dragonflies also go through incomplete metamorphosis. Unlike grasshoppers, their young don't resemble adults and don't live on land. Dragonfly young live underwater. These wingless nymphs are called naiads. Some naiads molt up to 17 times. To become an adult, the naiad climbs out of the water to shed its final skin and grow wings. Most species can fly within a few hours, though some need a week or more before they are strong enough to fly.

Naiads are carnivorous, just like adult dragonflies.

Spider Reproduction

Spider reproduction is more straightforward. The male deposits sperm on a spiderweb. The female then collects the sperm to fertilize her eggs. Females can lay thousands of eggs, which are placed in a cocoon called an egg sac. When the eggs hatch, the babies are fully formed spiders. Some females die after laying eggs. Some, such as the black widow spider, eat the male after fertilization.

Black widows can be identified by the red hourglass shape on the belly.

From Egg to Spider

A female spider lays up to a thousand eggs in a liquid that hardens when exposed to air.

The spider places her eggs in an egg sac, or cocoon, made of spider silk. Then she hides it in a safe place. Most spiders do not stay to care for their eggs.

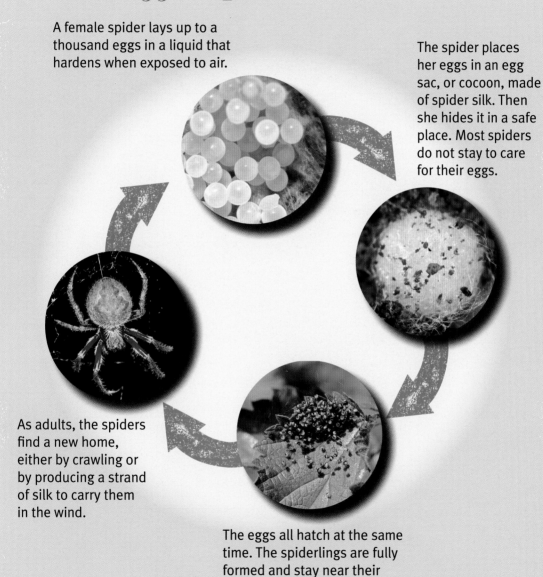

As adults, the spiders find a new home, either by crawling or by producing a strand of silk to carry them in the wind.

The eggs all hatch at the same time. The spiderlings are fully formed and stay near their cocoon until they are older.

Pesticides can eliminate some insect pests, but overuse may make the offspring immune to the chemicals.

CHAPTER 5

Friend or Foe?

The human race depends on many insect species for survival. Many insects eat other pest insects that damage crops. Insects are also a food source for many cultures. However, some insects pose a danger to humans. Bees pollinate plants, but their sting may cause a fatal allergic reaction in some people. Other insects are poisonous or help spread disease.

 Scientists estimate that less than 1 percent of all insect species are harmful.

Facing Hunger

Every decade, millions of locusts swarm African nations, devouring crops in areas suffering from drought. The United States may also be facing the threat of locust swarms. Mild winters and drought allow these insects to multiply rapidly. The insects can eat billions of dollars worth of crops, especially corn and soybeans.

Scientists are developing genetically modified seeds that are resistant to droughts and insects. Some people fear that these crops may be harmful to humans and other animals.

Locust is another name for a swarming grasshopper.

What's on the Menu?

Believe it or not, insects are a good source of nutrition. They contain a lot of protein—sometimes twice the protein found in fish. Many cultures eat insects as part of a regular diet. Grasshoppers are popular in Asia. Amazonian tribes regularly eat termites. Edible insects include caterpillars, worms, grubs, and beetles. Insects are easy to raise and an inexpensive substitute for meat. Scientists believe that insects may help reduce global starvation.

Disease

The recent warming of Earth's climate may increase the number of insects that spread blood-borne diseases to humans. Many insects, such as mosquitoes, thrive in warm, wet environments. Hotter, longer summers would give these insects plenty of opportunity to breed. Infected mosquitoes transmit malaria, which kills more than 1 million people each year. Fleas have transmitted plague throughout history. Now, plague has been found in the United States, though it is still extremely rare.

Special nets help protect people from disease-carrying mosquitoes.

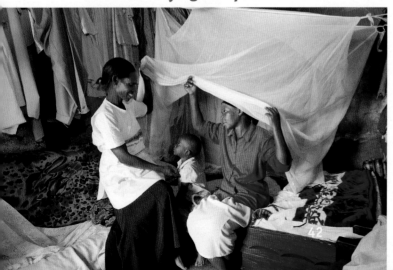

Only 1 of the more than 3,000 species of mosquitoes is known to carry malaria.

Army ant pincers can close a wound tightly.

Not All Bad

Some insects are useful in medical treatments. Doctors use army ant bites to close patients' wounds. Honey can help heal a skin rash. Some insects use saliva to keep their prey's blood from clotting. Those **enzymes** are leading to breakthroughs in human medicine.

Scientists face a difficult problem. Though many insects cause problems, others are helpful or even necessary to human survival. Experts are working to reduce dangerous insects without harming other insects, the environment, or people. ★

True Statistics

Length of the smallest insect: 0.008 in. (0.2 mm), fairyfly

Length of the largest insect: 4 in. (10.2 cm), giant weta

Weight of the heaviest insect: 2.5 oz. (71 g), giant weta

Longest life span of a spider: 20 years, tarantula

Longest life span of an insect: 17 years, periodical cicada

Shortest life span of an insect: 30 minutes, adult mayfly

Age of oldest known insect fossil: 400 million years

Age of oldest known flying insect fossil: 300 million years

Did you find the truth?

T Insects are a good source of nutrition.

F Spiders go through a process called metamorphosis.

Resources

Books

Bodden, Valerie. *Spiders*. Mankato, MN: Creative Education, 2011.

Murawski, Darlyne, and Nancy Honovich. *Ultimate Bugopedia: The Most Complete Bug Reference Ever*. Washington, DC: National Geographic Children's Books, 2013.

Visit this Scholastic Web site for more information on insects and spiders:

★ www.factsfornow.scholastic.com
Enter the keywords **Insects and Spiders**

Important Words

aerate (AYR-ate) — to supply with air

chitin (CHIH-tihn) — a hard, horny substance that forms part of the hard outer shell of insects, arachnids, and crustaceans

chrysalis (KRIS-uh-lis) — a hard outer shell where a butterfly or moth spends a quiet stage of development

enzymes (EN-zimez) — proteins produced by a plant or animal that cause chemical reactions to occur inside

exoskeleton (EK-soh-skeh-luh-tuhn) — an external supportive covering of an animal

genetically modified (juh-NET-ihk-lee MAH-duh-fide) — containing genes that have been changed in order to produce a desirable quality

larvae (LAR-vee) — insects at the stage of development between an egg and a pupa

metamorphosis (met-uh-MOR-fuh-sis) — a series of changes some animals go through as they develop into adults

naiads (NYE-ads) — the young forms of aquatic insects

nymph (NIMF) — the young form of an insect that goes through incomplete metamorphosis

pupa (PYOO-puh) —an insect in an inactive stage of development between a larva and an adult